Swan Lake

Jenny Dooley

Express Publishing

Published by Express Publishing
Liberty House, New Greenham Park,
Newbury, Berkshire RG19 6HW
Tel: (0044) 1635 817 363 – Fax: (0044) 1635 817 463
e-mail: inquiries@expresspublishing.co.uk
http://www.expresspublishing.co.uk

© Jenny Dooley, 1996

Design & Illustration © Express Publishing, 1996

Colour Illustrations: Nathan

First published 1996
Published in this edition 2006

Made in EU

ISBN-13: 978-1-84216-902-5
ISBN-10: 1-84216-902-5

Contents

Rocford

Odet

Zigfried

Odile

4

Prince Zigfried

Once upon a time, in a far away land, there lived a Prince. His name was Zigfried, and he was very unhappy. His father, the King, had died, and since then, everyone in the palace had forgotten how to smile. Without his father, Zigfried thought he would never feel happy again.

Every day, Zigfried sat at the window in his room in the palace, looking at the birds in the trees.

"How can they sing and fly so free? They must not feel like me."

His servant, Ozlowe, tried to make the Prince smile by telling him jokes or doing funny tricks for him. But the Prince would not smile.

"I know you love me Ozlowe, but I cannot smile. My heart is broken."

Ozlowe would not give up.

"Let's go for a walk, good Prince. Maybe we can find something outside which will make you happy."

"If you wish Ozlowe, but I don't think there's anything that can make *me* happy."

Ozlowe put on his hunting cap, and he took his crossbow. He enjoyed hunting and he hoped to catch a bird or a rabbit for the Prince.

They walked through the forest until they came to a lake. On the lake there was a beautiful white swan. It had a gold crown on its head, that only Princesses wear. The swan swam

towards the Prince and looked into his eyes. The swan's eyes were so sad that Prince Zigfried felt sorry for it.

"Here is a creature which feels worse than I do. But why do you have that crown on your head?"

The swan opened its wings and cried out.

"I think it's trying to tell me something."

Ozlowe had his crossbow in his hands. He wanted to shoot the swan.

"I'll get that swan for you, Prince. Just one minute."

"Ozlowe, no!"

Before Ozlowe could shoot, a magic owl flew from a tree and took Ozlowe's cap off his head. This cast a spell on him, and he was turned to stone. The Prince did not understand.

"Ozlowe, what's happened to you? Speak to me!"

He looked back at the lake. The swan was gone.

"Everything I do goes wrong. This must have happened because of me!"

The Prince returned to the palace sadder than before, thinking to himself:

"If only Ozlowe were here! There is nothing good in my life any more".

Zigfried's mother came to see him that night. She had something important to say.

"Zigfried, soon you will be eighteen years old. You must take your father's place as King. I am having a ball on your birthday so that you may choose a wife, and I will invite all the princesses from the other kingdoms."

"But I do not wish to marry, Mother. I do not love anyone."

"You will learn to love someone. First, you must stop thinking of yourself."

"If this will make you happy, I'll do it, Mother."

"It is not for *my* happiness that I am doing this. It is for yours, and all the other people in this land. You see, love is more powerful than we know. Without it, you will not be a great King."

His mother left him. He sat at the window, thinking of what she had said. He wanted to love someone with all his heart, but he didn't know who it would be.

The Beautiful Princess

On the morning of the Royal Ball, everybody was very busy in the palace. The Queen's maids were preparing the Queen's dress. The servants cleaned the floors and windows, and the cooks were cooking enough food for a thousand people.

The Prince looked handsome in his red outfit. But he was still not happy. He left the palace to be alone and think, and went to the stone statue of Ozlowe.

"It's my birthday today Ozlowe. I'm eighteen. That means that I must marry someone and become King. The problem is, I don't want to get married; I don't love anyone."

There was a quiet splashing in the lake. Zigfried looked and saw the beautiful swan with the gold crown.

"There it is! The beautiful swan has come back."

He went closer to the water to look at it. Its eyes had the same sadness in them, but it was happy to see Zigfried and it swam close to him. Zigfried looked into its eyes and talked to it.

"I think you understand me. I think you know how people feel."

A tear fell from the swan's eye.

"Don't cry. You should be happy that you are a swan. You will never have to marry someone you do not love. You will never feel sad when someone dies."

The swan made a loud cry. Its wings moved back and forth at its sides. Suddenly, an owl appeared as if from nowhere and flew at Zigfried's head, but it missed. The owl flew off, and the swan began to swim away.

"Wait. Don't leave."

Zigfried ran round the edge of the lake, following the swan. He had to run fast to see where it went. Soon, he was in a part of the forest he did not know. Tall trees blocked out the sun. It was very dark.

The swan swam to an ugly old castle. When it left the water, something magical happened; the swan turned into a beautiful Princess. She had long blonde hair and she wore a long white dress. The crown was still on her head. Zigfried ran to where she stood at the castle door.

"Wait! Where are you going?"

The Princess stopped, but she did not look at him.

"Look at me, please. My name is Prince Zigfried and I want to know who you are."

The Princess turned to look at the Prince. She had the same dark, sad eyes of the swan.

"My name is Princess Odile."

"But why were you a swan? Why do you look so sad?"

"An evil wizard called Rocford cast a spell on me. I may only leave the castle during the day as a swan."

"Where is this wizard? I will talk to him. I will tell him this is wrong."

"No, you mustn't. He will hurt you, I know. He does not want me to see another man."

"Tell me where this man is! I will fight him and free you."

"No, you must leave. He is dangerous."

"I won't leave until I see him; You must be set free."

"Please. You are very kind, but you must go away."

"I won't!"

She looked into his eyes again.

"If you want to do something for me, you will leave now."

"Odile, I will leave if you want me to. But I want you to come to the ball tonight. I must choose a wife and I want to choose you."

"I can't. The wizard won't let me."

"Find a way. Promise me you'll try."

She spoke, softly.

"All right, I'll try."

Odet

Zigfried left, and Odile went inside the castle. Odet, the wizard's evil daughter, was behind a tree. When she saw Odile talking to the Prince, she was jealous; she wanted to go to the ball, and what was more, she wanted to marry the Prince. She didn't like Odile, because she was so beautiful and kind. But the wizard loved her, so Odet couldn't do anything to hurt her...until now!

Odet went to the wizard's room, but he was not there. The room looked like a museum. There was an Egyptian statue against one wall, and large aquariums full of strange fish. On a table stood many different coloured bottles. Odet opened one of the bottles. Smoke came out of it. It smelled of burning wood.

The magic owl flew into the open window, unseen by Odet, and changed back into the wizard.

"Do you like the smell?"

"Oh, Father! You scared me."

"You wouldn't be afraid if you were not in my room when I wasn't here."

"I know father, but I have something very important to tell you. It's about Odile."

The wizard opened his eyes wide. He was a tall man, with a long, white beard and long, white hair. He wore a big black hat and a long black robe with stars on it.

"Tell me what you know!"

"First, you must promise to do something for me."

"What is it?"

"I can't tell you now. First, I must tell you about Odile, then I will ask for something. Will you do it?"

"Tell me, before I turn you into a frog!"

The wizard was very much in love with Odile. He would change his daughter into a frog because he wanted to know about Odile.

"Today, I saw Odile talking to Prince Zigfried. The Prince asked Odile to go to the royal ball tonight. He wants to marry her and free her from your evil powers."

The wizard turned in a circle and pointed his hand at the floor. Fire came from his fingers and hit the floor. The whole castle shook.

"I should have destroyed the Prince today, when I saw him with Odile."

"You saw him, too?"

"Yes, at the lake. I attacked him, but I was only an owl. Odile knew this and she left him. He must have followed her here."

"Oh yes Father, and he is so handsome! You should see his face!"

"Silence!"

The wizard turned himself into a large, stone ball. He threw himself against the walls, making the castle shake again. Alone in her room, Odile felt the castle shaking. She hid her head under a pillow on her bed; she hated it when the wizard got angry.

The wizard changed back into himself in his room.

"Now Father, you promised you'd do something for me."

"I never promised you anything!"

"Oh, Father. I want to go to the ball! I want to marry the Prince."

The wizard angrily raised his hand again. Then, he thought of something. Slowly, he lowered his hand.

"You would like to go to the ball, wouldn't you?"

"Oh yes, Father!"

"And you would like to marry the Prince?"

"Yes, I would."

"Then you will, and he will think that you are Odile."

"Oh Father, what a wonderful idea!"

She put her arms around him. His body was cold as stone, and his eyes were filled with fire.

A Bird in a Cage

Odile's room was at the top of the castle tower. Rocford had put her there, after he had taken her from her parents. She was the most beautiful Princess in the land, and her parents were good and kind. Rocford had asked her father if he could marry Odile.

"We must ask my daughter what she thinks."

Odile was brought to the wizard.

"Odile, this man has asked to marry you. He says he is very rich and that he will make you the happiest Princess in the world. What do you think?"

Odile looked into the wizard's eyes.

"Do you promise to love me forever, with all your heart? Will you love me so much that you will not think of what you want, even if it hurts you to do this?"

The look in her eyes and her questions made Rocford uncomfortable.

"Why do you ask me such questions? I told your father I could give you everything you could want."

The Princess smiled and turned her head away.

"I'm sorry Father, but I will not marry this man. He does not know what love is."

They did not know then that he was a wizard. Rocford had looked like a Prince. He wore beautiful clothes and looked very handsome. But, when he heard what Odile said to her

father, his face began to change. It became old and ugly. His clothes changed from blue to black.

"You don't know what you're saying, you silly girl. I do not have to ask for what I want. I am a wizard. I can do anything I please."

He waved his hands through the air, and a fire started in the castle where the Princess and her parents lived. He had turned Odile into a small bird in a cage, and carried her to his castle where he locked her up in a tower.

The entire kingdom was destroyed by this fire, and her parents were killed.

There was a real bird in a cage in Odile's room at the wizard's castle. The wizard had put it there so that Odile would remember the power he had over her. He only let her leave the castle as a swan because he did not want other men to fall in love with her. At night, she stayed in her room talking to the bird, who was her only friend. She called the bird Patrice, because it was her mother's name.

"Oh Patrice, what should I do? The ball is tonight, and I am a prisoner here. I believe the Prince loves me with all his heart. I saw it in his eyes. He loved me even as a swan."

The bird began moving its wings wildly. It always knew when something horrible was about to happen.

"What is it Patrice, what are you afraid of?"

Odile heard keys in her locked door. She put the bird and its cage behind a curtain, because she did not want the bird to see what was about to happen.

Odet's New Voice

The wizard entered Odile's room with Odet. Odet was the same age and height as Odile, but she had dark hair. However, she wasn't as beautiful as Odile, and this made her very jealous. The wizard spoke first.

"Sit down, Odile. I would like to ask you something."

The wizard waved his hand and a large and very comfortable pink chair appeared. Odile sat on it.

"Odet tells me that you would like to go to the ball tonight. Is that true?"

"Yes."

"If I let you go to this ball, will you promise to marry me?"

"I have told you, I will only marry a man who loves me and who I love."

"But you know I love you."

"If you loved me, you wouldn't keep me locked up in this castle. You wouldn't have killed my parents."

"You are a fool! Would you like to marry the Prince? Is that it?"

"He loves me more than you do."

"How do you know? He left you here with me. That shows you that you're wrong. He's afraid of me. He can't love you very much if he's afraid."

"He did it for me! I asked him to do it!"

"And did you tell him that you would go to the ball?"

"Yes."

"Then you lied. You knew I would not let you go."

"I said I would try. He knows that if I do not go it is not because I do not want to."

"And how does he know this?"

"You do not have to cast a spell on someone or make them rich to love you. You understand it by looking in their eyes. You know it by the way they speak and act."

"You are a dreamer!"

"And you have no heart!"

"Silence!"

The wizard raised both his arms and the castle shook. The curtain on the wall fell down, and the wizard saw the bird in the cage.

"Ah, the bird."

"If you hurt that bird you are worse than I thought."

The bird flew wildly as the wizard walked towards it. He picked up the cage.

"Now, why would I hurt this bird? It is like me. It has no heart. It does not feel anything when I do this."

The wizard pointed his fingers at Odet. She changed into Odile. She had the same blonde hair, the same eyes. She was even wearing the crown. Odile stood up.

"Tonight, Odet will go to the ball as you, Odile. Zigfried will marry her and we will see what true love is. Your hearts are nothing compared to my magic."

"You may look like me Odet, but there is something missing from your eyes. The Prince will know this."

"He does not love you Odile. He only loves what you look like."

"I almost forgot!"

The wizard waved his hand.

"Odet, say something."

When Odet spoke, she sounded just like Odile.

"Hello, Prince Zigfried. It's me, Odile. I love you."

Odile ran to her bed, crying. She fell on the bed and covered her face. Rocford laughed loudly. He took Odet out of the room and locked the door behind him. When Odile looked up, only the bird was with her. It too, had a tear in its eye.

The Ball

The ballroom in the palace was very big. There were hundreds of men and women dancing in the centre. Along the walls there were long white tables. They had candles and all kinds of food on them. At the top of the room, on a stage, were three large chairs. The Queen sat in the middle and Zigfried sat on her right. The chair on the left was empty. It was for the Princess who would be Zigfried's wife.

"Which Princess do you like the best?"

"The one I will choose is not here yet."

"But you have met them all, surely?"

"There is another one, mother, and she is a surprise. You will see."

Every time a new guest arrived, the ballroom doors were opened, and everyone fell silent. A servant called out the guests' names as they entered. Each time this happened, the Prince became very excited. But Odile never arrived.

It was almost twelve o'clock. Zigfried had promised his mother that he would choose a bride by midnight. The two large doors opened.

"Please, let it be her!"

It was a giant cake with 18 candles on it. Everyone in the room began to sing.

"Happy Birthday to you,
Happy Birthday to you,
Happy Birthday Prince Zigfried,
Happy Birthday to you!"

Zigfried and his mother walked towards the enormous cake.

"Now, make a wish and blow out all the candles."

No one heard him, but Zigfried said,

"I wish Odile would come and be my wife."

He blew out the candles and everyone cheered. The doors opened.

"Princess Odile."

It was Odet dressed as Odile. She wore a long white dress and long white gloves. The gold crown was shining on her head. She held a bouquet of flowers in her arms. She smiled as she walked towards the Queen and Prince. She gave the Queen the flowers, then bowed.

"Mother, this is Odile, the Princess I met in the forest."

"I knew your father. I'm sorry. I thought everyone had died in the fire. You must be the only one who lived."

Odet did not know what the wizard had done to Odile's parents. She stopped smiling.

"Oh Mother, her story is too sad to tell. Let us enjoy this evening together. We are her family now."

"Do you mean you wish to choose Princess Odile as your wife?"

"Yes, Mother, I do."

The Queen raised her hand for the men to sound their horns. Everyone was quiet.

"Ladies and gentlemen, I would like to announce the engagement of my son, Prince Zigfried. After tonight, he will be the King of this land, and he has chosen Princess Odile to be his wife."

Zigfried and Odet danced together. Everyone around them clapped their hands.

"Odile, I knew you would come. How did you escape from the evil wizard?"

"I ... I ran away."

"And he did not see you?"

The Prince stepped back so he could look at Odet's eyes. His heart sank when he saw those eyes. They looked like Odile's, but there was something missing in them. He didn't love her. Odet began to lie about her escape from Rocford.

"I saw a falling star in the sky. I closed my eyes and made a wish. When I opened them, I was in a carriage pulled by horses. That's how I got here. It must mean we're meant to be together. Oh Zigfried, tell me you will love me forever."

He held her close, because he did not want to look in her eyes. He knew he had loved Odile when he had first seen her. Now he didn't know. He thought there must be something wrong with him.

"Odile, I promise always to love you and never leave you."

Odile Escapes

Odile stood at her window, looking at the stars and the moon. There were bars at the window, but they were not necessary. Her window was high above a river. If she tried to escape, she would almost certainly fall into the water and die.

Her bird, Patrice, chirped behind her. She turned to look at the bird.

"Oh Patrice, I understand you. I am in a cage, too. But you must want to get out. I'm sorry I never thought of it. I have kept you locked up just like Rocford has kept *me* locked up. Because you are my only friend in this world, I wanted you to stay. But you must be free to fly."

Odile took the bird cage to the window. She opened its small door.

"Fly away, Patrice, and be free! Find another bird to love. It is the only thing worth living for."

The bird flew from its cage, through the bars on the window, into the night. Odile closed her eyes. She imagined that she was Patrice flying over the forest and lake. She flew into the garden of the palace. She landed on a palace wall and looked into a large window at the ball. Beautiful women in beautiful dresses were dancing with handsome men.

She saw the Prince with his mother and the cake with the eighteen candles. Then, Odet entered the room dressed as her. When she opened her eyes, she found to her amazement

that she *was* outside the palace window. When she had set the bird free, she had also set herself free. Because she believed with all her heart in love and freedom, everything that she imagined came true.

The wizard knew that Odile hated him, and it made him angry. He wanted to make her love him, so he decided to have a ball for her. Using his magic, he made a large room full of people dancing. He changed himself into a young man again, the same young man he was when he had taken Odile from her parents.

He went to her room with flowers. He knocked on her door.

"Odile, I have a surprise for you."

There was no answer. He couldn't even hear the bird.

"Odile, it's me, Rocford. I've decided to take you to a ball."

When there was no answer and he heard nothing, he became angry. He made the door disappear. His anger turned him back into the old, evil man that he was. He saw the bird cage on the floor. The room was empty. Roaring with anger, he turned himself into an owl and flew from the castle towards the palace.

The Prince
chases the Princess

When Odile saw Odet dancing with Zigfried, she ran to the palace entrance. The guards stopped her.

"Who are you?"

"My name is Princess Odile. The Prince is expecting me."

"No. Princess Odile has already entered. You must be lying."

"Please, you must believe me. That is not Princess Odile. She is lying."

But the guards wouldn't believe her. She ran back to the window and knocked hard on it. Everyone turned to look at her. The Prince could not believe what he saw - two Odiles. He looked at Odet.

"What is going on?"

"I don't know. The evil wizard must have changed someone to look like me."

Odile kept knocking on the window. She was crying. Zigfried could now see that she had the same eyes as the swan. Rocford flew down next to Odile as the owl. He held her in both arms.

"Did you think you could escape from me?"

The Prince ran from the ballroom. He saw Odile fighting with the wizard.

"Take your hands off her, Rocford."

Rocford let go of Odile's arms.

"I should have killed you that day at the lake. But I will be happy to do it now."

The wizard lifted up his hand. Odile stopped him.

37

"Wait! Don't do it. I'll go with you. I'll do what you want. Just don't hurt him."

"Odile, what are you saying? Don't leave me again!"

She could not look at him, because if she did, she would not want to leave.

"I'm doing this for us. If you die, I will die with you. It is better for us to live and hope to be together one day."

Odet ran out of the palace. She still looked like Odile.

"Who is this, then?"

"It is Odet, the wizard's evil daughter. She only looks like me. Look into her eyes and you will know."

"I knew it."

Odet also had magical powers. She changed herself back to her real body.

"It is too late Zigfried. You promised to marry me and love me forever. If you do not keep this promise, you will never be able to keep another."

Odet changed herself into a bird. The wizard was an owl and Odile was a swan. They flew together away from the palace, back to Rocford's castle. The Queen and many others came out of the palace to see what had happened. Zigfried went after Odile.

"Guards, bring me my horse."

"Zigfried, where are you going? Where is the Princess?"

"She has gone away, Mother, and I must find her."

The guards brought the Prince a beautiful white horse, and gave him his sword.

"Do you want us to call the men, Your Highness?"

"No, this is something I must do alone."

"Zigfried, do not leave the palace alone. If something happens to you, we will be without a King. It is your duty to stay with me!"

"Mother, being a King means nothing if you are not with the woman you love. I would rather die than leave Odile with that evil wizard."

The Prince spurred his horse on and rode quickly towards the dark forest.

41

The Fire

Rocford, Odet and Odile flew onto the tower of the castle. They changed back into people. Odile was weeping loudly. The wizard just laughed his evil laugh and said:

"Odile, now I know how to get you to marry me. If you don't, I will kill the Prince, and you will watch him die."

"Father, you do not have to kill Zigfried. He has already promised to marry me. He cannot break such a promise."

"Neither of you has a heart. How can you ever expect to be happy if you know that someone does not love you? But you will see. Love is stronger than spells. You will never succeed in getting what you want."

At this, they saw Zigfried coming towards the castle on his horse.

"We shall see which is stronger, love or hate!"

The wizard made a wall of fire appear in front of Zigfried. Zigfried could only think of Odile. He rode right through the fire without getting hurt.

Odile said triumphantly:

"You see. I am right."

As she ran from the wizard, he tried to block her way by making the doors close in front of her. But Odile just ran faster and escaped through each one.

The Prince saw Odile on the steps going up to the tower. He took her in his arms.

"Odile, I will never let you leave me again. Say that you will stay with me forever."

"I will! I will! I love you Zigfried!"

The wizard appeared at the top of the steps. Odet was behind him.

"You will not escape death this time, Zigfried."

The Prince took out his sword. Odile tried to stop him.

"Do not fight him, Zigfried. If he kills you, I will lose everyone I've ever loved."

"You are right Odile. Zigfried is only a boy. He is no match for me. Now, come back to your room, and let this little boy go home to his mother."

"Rocford, your words will not discourage me. I would kill you now, but I will give you one last chance to live. Let us leave in peace and never come near Odile again."

"You really *are* a little boy if you think that you can harm me."

Rocford raised his hand, and Odile flew through the air to where Odet stood. Zigfried ran at Rocford and tried to stab him with his sword. Rocford put his hand up. The sword touched it and turned into water. Without a sword, Zigfried attacked the wizard. Rocford threw Zigfried down the steps. He picked up a stick and turned it into a sword. He pointed it at Zigfried's heart as he lay on the ground.

"Rocford! Don't!"

"Say you will marry me Odile, and I will let him live."

"Don't do it Odile! Don't make yourself more unhappy just for me!"

The wizard prodded Zigfried with the sword.

"And you have promised to marry me, Zigfried. You said you would always love me."

"I said that because I thought you were Odile. I would never marry you. I would rather die."

Zigfried took the wizard's sword and pushed it deep into his own heart.

"Zigfried, no!"

Something strange began to happen. The castle began to shake. Large stones fell from the ceiling, and Rocford and Odet were killed. Odile ran to Zigfried. She took the sword out of his heart and pulled his body out of the castle, before it fell to the ground.

The Wedding

Dawn broke in the forest, but no birds sang. The castle was nothing but a pile of stones. The only sound was Odile crying over Zigfried's body.

"Oh Zigfried, my one true love! Why did you have to die?"

At this, the Prince opened first one eye, then the other.

"You're alive! Oh, Zigfried!"

She hugged the Prince and cried tears of happiness.

"I love you, Odile. I knew that my love was stronger than that sword. Nothing is more powerful than a person's heart. Tell me you will marry me, and I will love you forever."

"Of course I will Zigfried. You have made my dreams come true. We were right to believe in love!"

They left the old castle together on Zigfried's horse. When they came to the lake near the palace, they saw Ozlowe. He was not a statue anymore. He stood, scratching his head. All of the wizard's spells had been broken when he died. The Prince was full of joy.

"Ozlowe!"

"Master Zigfried, I don't know what happened. I was standing here about to shoot a swan and ... "

"That will teach you never to kill anything. This is Princess Odile. She was the swan you tried to kill."

Ozlowe was very confused.

"Prince Zigfried, I think I'd better go to bed. I don't feel very well."

When the servants and the Queen heard about Zigfried and Odile's marriage, there was a big celebration. All the people in the land and the surrounding kindoms were invited to the wedding. It took place at the edge of the lake, where Zigfried had first seen Odile.

Odile wore a beautiful long wedding dress. Zigfried's mother walked towards them.

"Zigfried, I want you to know that what you did was right. Though I asked you to stay at the palace, you left for a better reason. You should always follow your heart, especially when it is full of love. Your father would be very proud of you."

Zigfried's mother was so happy that she had tears in her eyes. The Prince took Odile's hands. They stood together in front of the lake. The Queen put the King's crown on Zigfried's head. The priest spoke to the new King and Queen.

"Marriage is a wonderful thing. And what makes this marriage special is that the love you have for each other will affect everyone in this land. Through your happiness, we will become happy. Through your love for each other, we will love each other. Is this what you want? Is your love strong enough to lead a land of people who need joy in their lives?"

Odile spoke first.

"It is."

"Of course, it is!"

"Then by the power that is given to me by God, I pronounce you husband and wife."

At that moment a joyful chirp was heard and a little bird flew from a rose bush and sat on Odile's hand.

"Patrice, my little friend! You're back!"

Then Odile turned to Zigfried and said:

"You see my beloved King, love is stronger than anything in this world. When you love somebody or something you never lose them."

Zigfried looked lovingly into his bride's eyes, they kissed and everybody cheered.

Word List

any more (phr)
ball (n)
be gone (phr)
be turned to stone
    (phr)
cap (n)
cast a spell on sb (phr)
catch (caught-caught)
    (v)
choose (chose-chosen)
    (v)
come (came-come) (v)
creature (n)
crossbow (n)
crown (n)
cry out (phr v)
enjoy (v)
far-away (adj)
feel (felt-felt) (v)
feel sorry for sb (phr)
fly (flew-flown) (v)
forest (n)
forget (forgot-
    forgotten) (v)
free (adj)
give up (gave-given)
    (phr v)
hope (v)
hunting (adj/n)
if only (phr conj)
important (adj)
invite (v)

joke (n)
just one minute (phr)
kingdom (n)
lake (n)
land (n)
leave (left-left) (v)
marry (v)
once upon a time
    (phr)
one's heart is broken
    (phr)
owl (n)
palace (n)
powerful (adj)
prince (n)
princess (n)
put on (put-put)
    (phr v)
servant (n)
shoot (shot-shot) (v)
since then (phr)
sit (sat-sat) (v)
smile (v)
speak (spoke-spoken)
    (v)
sth goes wrong (phr)
swan (n)
swim (swam-swum) (v)
take sb's place (phr)
think (thought-
    thought) (v)
towards (prep)
trick (n)
try (v)

wear (wore-worn) (v)
wife (n)
wing (n)
wish (v)
with all one's heart
    (phr)

alone (adj)
appear (v)
as if (phr conj)
away (adv)
back and forth (phr)
become (became-
    become) (v)
block out (phr v)
blonde (adj)
busy (adj)
castle (n)
close to (phr prep)
come back (phr v)
dangerous (adj)
during (prep)
edge (n)
evil (adj)
fall (fell-fallen) (v)
fight (fought-fought)
    (v)
follow (v)
free (v)
get married (phr)
go away (went-gone)
    (phr v)

51

handsome (adj)
hurt (hurt-hurt) (v)
let (let-let) (v)
look (v)
maid (n)
make a loud cry (phr)
miss (v)
move (v)
outfit (n)
prepare (v)
promise (v)
royal (adj)
run (ran-run) (v)
sadness (n)
same (adj)
set free (phr)
side (n)
softly (adv)
splashing (n)
stand (stood-stood) (v)
statue (n)
stone (adj)
tear (n)
turn into (phr v)
ugly (adj)
way (n)
wizard (n)
wrong (adj)

Chapter 3

against (prep)
angrily (adv)
aquarium (n)
attack (v)
be (very much) in love
    with sb (phr)

beard (n)
burning (adj)
change back into (phr)
coloured (adj)
come out of (v)
destroy (v)
Egyptian (adj)
filled with (adj)
frog (n)
get angry (phr)
hate (v)
hide (hid-hidden) (v)
hit (hit-hit) (v)
jealous (adj)
look like (v)
lower (v)
museum (n)
open one's eyes wide
    (phr)
pillow (n)
point one's hand at
    sth (phr)
power (n)
put one's arms around
    sb (phr)
raise (v)
robe (n)
scare (v)
shake (shook-shaken)
    (v)
silence (n)
smell of
    (smelled/smelt-
    smelled/smelt (v)
smoke (n)
throw oneself against
    (phr)

unseen (adj)
what is more (phr)
whole (adj)
wonderful (adj)
wood (n)

Chapter 4

a fire starts (phr)
be afraid of (phr)
bring (brought-
    brought) (v)
cage (n)
carry (v)
curtain (n)
entire (adj)
even (adv)
fall in love with sb
    (phr)
have power over sb
    (phr)
horrible (adj)
lock sb up (phr v)
please (v)
prisoner (n)
silly (adj)
stay (v)
sth is about to happen
    (phr)
such (det)
the look in one's eyes
    (phr)
tower (n)
turn one's head away
    (phr)
uncomfortable (adj)

wave one's hands
   through the air
   (phr)
wildly (adv)

Chapter 5

act (v)
almost (adv)
be wrong (phr)
compared to (phr-
   prep)
cover (v)
dark (adj)
dreamer (n)
enter (v)
fool (n)
height (n)
however (adv)
Is that true? (phr)
keep (kept-kept) (v)
laugh (v)
lie (v)
look up (phr)
loudly (adv)
pick up (phr v)
sound like (v)
there's sth missing
   (phr)
true (adj)
voice (n)

Chapter 6

announce (v)
arrive (v)
ballroom (n)

blow out (blew-blown)
   (phr v)
bouquet (n)
bow (v)
bride (n)
call out (phr v)
candle (n)
carriage (n)
cheer (v)
clap one's hands (phr)
dressed as (adj)
empty (adj)
engagement (n)
enormous (adj)
escape (v)
excited (adj)
fall silent (phr)
falling star (n)
giant (adj)
guest (n)
hold sb close (phr)
horn (n)
let it be (phr)
make a wish (phr)
meet (met-met) (v)
midnight (n)
my heart sank (exp)
pull (v)
run away (phr v)
shine (shone-shone)
   (v)
sound (v)
stage (n)
step back (phr v)
sth was meant to be
   (phr)
surely (adv)

surprise (n)
together (adv)

Chapter 7

bar (n)
be worth doing sth
   (phr)
certainly (adv)
chirp (v)
come true (phr)
disappear (v)
freedom (n)
get out (got-got) (phr
   v)
imagine (v)
knock at/on (v)
land (v)
necessary (adj)
roar with anger (phr)
to one's amazement
   (phr)

Chapter 8

call (v)
chase (v)
duty (n)
entrance (n)
expect sb (v)
go after (phr v)
guard (n)
keep a promise (phr)
lift up (phr v)
ride (rode-ridden) (v)
spur on (v)
sword (n)

take one's hands off sb (phr)

What's going on? (phr)

would rather (phr modal v)

Your Highness (exp)

Chapter 9

be a match for sb (phr)

be right (phr)

block one's way (phr)

break a promise (phr)

ceiling (n)

chance (n)

death (n)

discourage (v)

get hurt (phr)

ground (n)

harm (v)

hate (n)

in peace (phr)

lie (lay-lain) (v)

lose (lost-lost) (v)

neither of (pron)

point at (v)

prod (v)

push (v)

right (adv)

stab (v)

step (n)

stick (n)

succeed in (v)

take out (took-taken) (phr v)

through (prep)

triumphantly (adv)

weep (wept-wept) (v)

Chapter 10

affect (v)

alive (adj)

be back (was/were-been) (phr v)

be nothing but (phr)

be proud of sb (phr)

beloved (adj)

break a spell (phr)

celebration (n)

confused (adj)

cry over sb/sth (phr)

dawn breaks (phr)

especially (adv)

follow one's heart (exp)

hear about sth (heard-heard) (v)

hug (v)

husband (n)

joy (n)

joyful (adj)

kiss (v)

lead (led-led) (v)

lovingly (adv)

marriage (n)

pile (n)

priest (n)

pronounce (v)

reason (n)

rose bush (n)

scratch (v)

sound (n)

special (adj)

surrounding (adj)

take place (phr)

wedding (n)

wedding dress (n)